MW00745574

UNDERSTAND WEALTH

What You Have in Common with All Wealthy People

Copyright © 2022

The views and opinions expressed in this book
are those of the author and do not necessarily
reflect the official policy or position of any other
agency, organization, employer or company.

This book is not intended to provide
personalized legal, accounting, financial or
investment advice. It is suggested that readers
seek the counsel of competent professionals
with regard to such matters as interpretation of
the law, proper accounting procedures, tax
preparation, financial planning and investment
strategies. The author and publisher specifically
disclaim any liability, loss, or risk which is
incurred as a consequence, directly or
indirectly, of the use and application of any of
the contents in this work.

All rights reserved. No part of this book may be
used, reproduced or transmitted in any form or
by any means whatsoever except in the case of
brief quotations embodied in critical articles and
reviews without written permission from the
author.

CONTENTS

PREFACE

When I learned how to Think Wealthy, I saved my life.

That may sound dramatic, but when you get completely out of debt for the first time in your life, fully fund your retirement accounts, know you will never again have crushing financial stress and you become known as the "rich uncles" in your family, you have achieved more financial milestones than you ever dreamed were possible.

When I learned how to Think Wealthy, I saved my life because I was finally able to breathe. I was finally able to pause and really plan the life that I wanted to live — not the life that a boss or employer wanted for me.

This is the book series I wish someone had given to me in high school, in college and every five years after that so I could have started my adult life on the strongest financial footing possible. Had I known then what I know now I would've been even MORE financially independent...just so, so much earlier.

Perhaps I can right that wrong for future generations.

This is the 2nd book in my 6-part "Think Wealthy" series that I wrote based on ongoing conversations with friends and family about how to achieve financial independence.

Growing up as I did in my close Midwestern family, rich and wealthy people were always put on a pedestal, admired on one hand and mildly resented and feared on the other. I had some MAJOR work to do to retrain my brain for allowing the money I made (or collected as we'll later see) to flow through me for a higher purpose of creating safety, security and, ultimately, financial freedom in my life.

Financial independence may bring to mind for you millions or billions of dollars of assets in acquired wealth or it may simply mean putting a foolproof system in place that produces the monthly cash flow you need for the rest of your life without the need for first minting a mountain of cash. (The FIRE Movement is one version of this.) Either is valid as they both provide a different path to financial independence, each with their unique advantages and disadvantages.

Many thanks to my amazing friends and family who have supported and informed this labor of love.

I hope you enjoy this book series as much as I enjoyed writing it!

OUR ONLY FINANCIAL JOB IN LIFE

Our only financial job in life is to pay our monthly bills until game over.

That's it.

Even billionaires have monthly bills – and lots of them!

How do we pay our monthly bills after schooling ends, on through our years in the workforce and all the way through what might be decades of retirement?

If you've got that all figured out, then this book series will keep you "in the conversation" and motivated toward financial independence and/or more wealth creation.

For most people reading these books, however, you were raised in families that approached this financial job of ours by thinking about it month-to-month – I JUST clear the hurdle of affording one month before I start planning (and worrying) about the next month – which is a very middle class approach – and which is fine if that's all you've ever known like me.

The KEY to successful personal finance, however, is to learn to think and to plan year-to-year, to have a longer time horizon in mind. To do that is to Think Wealthy, which is the sole purpose of the words I'm stacking next to each other in all the books in this series.

If just ONE of these books can actually shift your thinking from scrambling week-to-week or month-to-month to confidently flowing from YEAR-to-YEAR, then you're well on your way to creating wealth and financial independence for you and your family for generations to come.

I kid you not – for generations to come.

It'd be my absolute honor to help you get there.

INTRODUCTION

You're awesome!

How's that for an introduction?

You are awesome because you already have everything you need inside to create financial independence one day for you and your family. The financial puzzle pieces are all there, you just need to solve it as you learn to Think Wealthy.

Personally, I could have avoided YEARS of student loan and credit card debt if only someone would have taught me how to think wealthy sooner.

You can LEARN to be wealthy or financially independent – or BOTH – because the rules by which you make money and your MONEY makes money are simple and only need to be learned once.

I'm living proof of that.

I went from being the poorest guy in any room to a self-made first-generation millionaire and I'm going to show you how I did it.

There are plenty of great financial planners out there and they are easy enough to hire (and you SHOULD hire one at some point), but what has protected me and my family and what will protect YOU, too, in the long run is for you to "get it" – for you to "get" money. Because once you get it, you got it…and you'll never forget it.

Once you "get it"…once you understand money and wealth…you'll never have to learn it again.

Tell me if this sounds familiar…

No one ever shared with you everything they knew about money – how money works in the world, what it's really for and, most importantly, how to make as much of it as you want in your lifetime – I never heard it from my parents, grandparents, teachers and I'm guessing you never heard it, either.

Sucks to be just the two of us, right?

Turns out it's a LOT more than just the two of us because nearly 80% of Americans live paycheck-to-paycheck which means they don't "get" money yet, either!

80% of Americans or over 100 million people live paycheck to paycheck in the wealthiest country the world has ever known – SAY WHAT?

If misery loves company then there's a big 'ol party going on in the U.S. of A.

Which is exactly why I am writing these books. So we can stop commiserating in our negative net worth and start celebrating our financial freedom TOGETHER.

My Goal of Zero Net Worth

For years my highest financial aspiration was to simply break even and have a net worth of zero.

I can't believe I'm sharing that. It's so ridiculous.

I LITERALLY used to dream about having no debt and no assets to my name. "What a financial god I'll be when I finally have ZERO dollars to my name instead of all this debt! I'm going to shout it from the rooftops and people will dance behind me as I'm asked to lead endless parades around town."

My life's highest financial goal for the longest time was to JUST BREAK EVEN in the financial game of life.

Silly, goofy money-unsavvy Todd. Now that we have our retirement years accounted for, the memory stings a little bit less, but it's still embarrassing to admit.

But you know what? How many people reading this right now might have the exact same financial goal that I did? "Man, if I can just get to ZERO net worth, I'll be better off than everyone I know!"

All I had heard from my parents and teachers was to get good grades and work hard and that the financial stuff would take of itself.

That was a lie.

The financial stuff does NOT just take care of itself...at least not without understanding how money works in the world and how YOU can make it work hard for you in your own life.

From Poorest Guy in Any Room to 1st Generation Millionaire

I'll keep the details of my life to a relative minimum as we're here to talk about

YOU, but suffice it to say that since college I have found relative success in many different areas of the fickle, über-competitive entertainment industry in Hollywood, sticking with a particular career only until it no longer paid emotional dividends.

In terms of education, I double-majored in Linguistics and French in undergrad and was a graduate student at the USC School of Cinema-Television. I worked in commercial casting, I was a successful commercial actor appearing in spots for Volkswagen, Subway, Sears, Westin Hotels, Men Are From Mars Women Are From Venus board game and on and on..., I was a reality TV casting manager traveling the country for MTV before transitioning to a Director of Marketing and Account Director role for a digital creative agency that worked with all the major movie studios and premium cable channels to help them market their shows and movies online through any digital channel and platform we could think of. Most recently I have worked as the Head of Growth for an awesome boutique branding agency based in the L.A. area.

I was also a film projectionist for a work-study job in college (did you ever see *Cinema Paradiso*?) and then to some of the wealthiest and most famous of the Hollywood elite. I used to drive to people's homes in Beverly Hills, BelAir, Pacific Palisades, Malibu...homes worth tens and even hundreds of millions of dollars to project 35-millimeter prints of the latest films in their private screening rooms. (Before the digital revolution hit its tipping point and everyone started just pushing buttons at home.)

What's a few hundred dollars they would pay me for an in-home film screening of the newest releases when you're not paying that crazy upcharge on popcorn and soda at the theater, amirite?

I used to peek out from the port windows at the lavish screening rooms filled with popcorn machines and endless jars filled to the brim with candy and think, "What is so different between them and me? What

do they know about money that I don't?
And how do I get to THAT side of life?"

Financially-speaking, I've had windfalls of
money roll in over the years from
commercial residual checks, I've been
unemployed and collecting
unemployment for months at a time in-
between reality casting gigs and I have
humbly and frugally lived with a stable
six-figure income, replete with 401k and
quarterly sales bonuses.

Through all those careers and adventures
I have seen both sides of the coin, having
nothing to my name for decades when I
was easily the poorest guy in any room,
to seeing how "the other half" lived in
their amazing mansions and now to
making a beeline straight for a wealthy,
happy and healthy life for myself and my
family.

My partner and I have gone from a
negative net worth of over $50,000 when
we met fifteen years ago to being
squarely on track to become 1st
generation millionaires.

We have zero debt and our FICO scores are well into the 800s. Life ain't bad on the financial front...and it's only getting better.

And yet, none of this would have been possible if I didn't learn how to Think Wealthy. Swing a dead cat (as the saying goes) and you could easily hit another couple with all the same life circumstances but who are now even MORE in debt.

What's the difference between us and them?

Welcome to the Think Wealthy Series

I'm fascinated by what's called the psychology of wealth...the idea that simply how you THINK about money directly affects how much money you HAVE.

Yet it's absolutely true.

Regardless of how much I struggled to be better with my money than my parents were, for years (and years and years) I just barely got by.

Just like them.

Saddled with consumer debt I lived paycheck to paycheck just like my parents always did (and the 80% of the rest of Americans).

But who could blame my parents? If they knew better they would have shared it with me and my sister, too – they only want the best for us, right?

The U.S. is always touted as the wealthiest nation ever to exist in the modern era – but if we can't create and pass down our collective financial wisdom to successive generations, we don't deserve to hang onto that title for much longer.

What we're talking about in this book is having it ALL – more financial means than you need in one lifetime (if you want), an inner confidence against whatever life tries to throw your way (did I mention yet that I was diagnosed with cancer in March of 2021? #lifehappens), being surrounded by a supportive, loving family and a wealth of true friends who get you and who inspire you (and whom you inspire) to be ever better people in the world.

That's what I call WELL-ROUNDED WEALTH and it's what I want for you and your family – we'll talk more about this in the final book in the series.

I didn't realize it at the time, for those decades of early adulthood, but debt made me feel LESS THAN in life – it made me feel that I actually had less VALUE as a human being than other people…and that I certainly had less value than anyone with the appearance of financial success.

For years and years I mistakenly confused my NET WORTH with my SELF WORTH and as a wide-eyed man-child buried under $60,000 of consumer debt from student loans and credit cards who was entering the labor force, I made way too many mistakes that actually kept me from growing up financially (and emotionally) – it was a diaper of debt.

Are you, too, wearing a diaper of debt? (I may be the first Financial Poet Laureate!)

As you can imagine, now that I've figured it out for myself, I'm over-the-moon excited to talk about money with everyone else.

I love the peace of mind and the sense of safety, security and freedom that having money in the bank has afforded us. Heck, it created the space for me to not just TALK about this book (everyone has a book or ten in them), but actually sit down and WRITE it.

I wish I had read this book in high school before going to college and then again as I headed out into the world as a young pup (with the saddest excuse for a moustache the world has ever seen).

I also wish I had this book at my disposal when I needed to be reminded of how powerful I was in creating my OWN life and doing it with confidence and purpose.

The biggest gift you can give yourself, and my singular goal in writing these books, is for you to be confident with your money because it will mean you are also confident with the decisions in most every other area of your life.

Besides, I've done the bulk of the work in writing it down – all you have to do is READ the dern thing and think about yourself!

The Goal of This Think Wealthy Book Series

My singular goal in writing this book series is to change your entire relationship with money.

For the better.

Forever.

(I like to aim low.)

And we're going to have fun along the way because life just isn't as serious as we've made it out to be.

By the end of these books, if I've done my job, you will be excited about money, creating more of it, investing it, donating it...letting it flow through you to do good and make even MORE MONEY in the world.

And you'll do it all in good conscience so you can sleep soundly at night.

I envision a country whose citizens aren't on the collective brink of collapse, where its people AND its government don't spend above their means.

It sickens me that the majority of Americans do not have even a spare $1,000 in a bank account, that they don't know that they SHOULD have it tucked away and understand WHY – it should scare the bejeezus out of all of us.

Luckily for you and for anyone who dares to crack the digital pages of this book, there are only a few timeless facts about money and wealth you need to learn. If you don't have these basics at the very center of your financial worldview informing the money decisions you make day in and day out, you'll probably never make a lot of money…or at least you certainly won't KEEP much of it.

I'm proud of my Midwestern heritage – I just wish it didn't take me 40 years to figure out the basic financial concepts of wealth creation and wealth management.

Before we dig into what the wealthy already know about money, let's take any of the sting out of the word "wealth" first.

Do you want to be wealthy?

You scream, "YES!" in your mind, but then shrink back because you may not know anyone who IS wealthy and it feels greedy when you're surrounded by friends and family who are always struggling to get by. Or maybe it sounds too hoity-toity to be wealthy and you just want to keep it real, yo. Or whatever other of a thousand negative responses you may have associated with the word "wealth."

To me, wealth is simply having MORE money tomorrow than you have today. That's it.

Wealth is nothing more than having more money tomorrow than you have today.

Wealth is having a higher net worth tomorrow than you do today.

Not a million dollars more – but even five dollars more – each day – quickly adds up.

So do you want to be wealthy – do you want to have progressively more money day after day?

If you are tired of throwing your monthly bills across the room to hit the snooze button on the life you've always wanted, then let's grab a virtual cup of joe or an awesome craft beer (it must be 5pm somewhere right now) and let's figure this out together.

The point of this second book in the Personal Finance series is to pull back the curtain on wealth and help us get out of our own way and our past conditioning to see it for what it really is.

Everyone who wants to think wealthy, please turn the page...now!

WHAT IS WEALTH?

As excited as I was to talk about money in _Understand Money_, the first step in the Think Wealthy Personal Finance book series, you can imagine that my eyes are teetering on the edge of their sockets now that we're talking about WEALTH.

That one word inspires me into action day after day after day, but maybe not for the reasons you'd think.

Wealth of anything is just an abundance of that thing - it is a great quantity, a plentiful amount - and while this book series is called Think Wealthy because we are focusing on financial enrichment with money as the fuel for feeling safe, secure and free in our lives, it's important to remember the importance of wealth in ALL areas of a well-rounded life.

What good is a mountain of growing financial assets if you don't have the loving support of family and friends, children who enjoy spending time with you, peer relationships with people you respect and admire and strong mental and physical health for you to actually enjoy your wealth?

Of course, "wealth" is back to being a dirty word these days. People may cheer the success of a newfound millionaire or billionaire for proving the American Dream we all hope to achieve, but at what expense we have to acknowledge. When the wealthy have significantly INCREASED their net worth as world economies shut down and sputter back to life in the global COVID-19 pandemic while millions have lost their jobs (their careers, their loved ones, even) and many are months behind on rent or mortgage payments, the system seems rigged.

As I stated in the first book in this series, _Understand Money_, we won't be looking at money and wealth at a macro level, however, as my focus is on you, the reader, the person responsible for navigating your own financial waters. I'm not denying the very real inequalities that exist in the United States of America and the disparity that has continued to grow unchecked for decades now, I'm merely concentrating on you and your family to help you create lives in which you feel safe, secure and free so that you can concentrate on learning, growing and helping out others where you can.

Back on topic, we're going to spend this entire book unpacking what it means to be wealthy.

Be careful, though, not to confuse wealth with EXCESS.

Excess is TOO MUCH of something… kind of like when Kanye (now officially Ye) speaks at an awards show…whereas wealth is limitless abundance.

Wealth is limitless abundance. Excess, on the other hand, is *too much* of something.

This is the difference between a family who has rather quietly kept financial wealth flowing throughout the generations by learning how to diversify their investments and grow their pool of wealth versus a family that is suddenly blessed (or cursed) by winning the lottery and they make every wrong decision feeling the excess of money they've been handed.

Also, let's not confuse financial wealth with materialism (as we saw in the first book) because HAVING money and SPENDING money are two totally different animals, really a MEOW and a MOO comparison. Yet, still many people conflate those two ideas and pay dearly for it.

This is a BIG ONE to grasp if you grew up with nothing…wealth does not (necessarily) equal the buying of things or the buying of more stuff than you need.

Wealth and materialism are NOT the same thing.

You can live exactly as you do right now with either $10 or $10,000,000 dollars to your name – the choice of HOW YOU LIVE is always yours to make.

My mom would often respond to the idea of financial fortune with her customary, "What would I DO with a million dollars? I HAVE more than I need as it is."

Not that a million dollars signifies real wealth any longer, but the larger mental mistake that she would make is that having more money meant that she would have to purchase more things. She was an educator, a savvy accountant and an incredible mother who always craved financial security, yet she never understood the value, the power, even, of money just sitting in a bank for safety's sake and invested in a diverse portfolio for a feeling of long-term security.

As my parents have aged up, I have taken over the responsibility of handling all of their finances and although they may have a house full of things (not TOO many, thank God – they never became hoarders), they have always skated on the razor's edge of financial insolvency. I saw how they struggled to make ends meet and how they both admired and deeply envied anyone who had more financial resources than they did and it took me years to separate the two concepts of wealth and materialism.

In theory (and in practice), most millionaires look like your neighbors. In fact, they very possibly ARE your neighbors. I don't mean mega-millionaires, but people living what appears to be an average lifestyle without the need for the glitz and glamor that we so often associate with celebrities and wealthy people who live their lives in the public eye.

In terms of the personal wealth that any of us can achieve, we can have a wealth of friends, a wealth of love and support from our family, wealth of happiness and excitement when we're in love, spiritual wealth when we tithe at church to guarantee our spot in heaven – kidding! – I know Martin Luther already cleared this one up with the Reformation, but talk about VALUE for your money, you could literally BUY your way into heaven! (Or so people thought.)

And, of course, a person can be wealthy without having any dough in the bank, too.

Let's say someone who donates all of their time and energy to a non-profit that benefits the homeless and is only paid minimum wage, but impacts hundreds or thousands of lives – they can certainly be considered wealthier on one level than the man or woman who amasses millions of dollars in the bank but is never emotionally available to their family or who never gives a dime to charity from their heart.

Remember, there will always be financially wealthy people who are unfulfilled, miserable SOBs since money just makes you more of who you already are.

It should be a great relief to learn that money only AMPLIFIES your core values (or lack thereof) – which supports our upcoming conversation that wealth of MONEY and wealth of HAPPINESS are not one and the same.

My personal goal and our collective goal together during our Tilt-A-Whirls around the sun, then, is to have wealth in ALL areas of our lives.

That's what I call **well-rounded wealth** (oh, what the heck, I might as well annoy one more Amazon reviewer with my all caps love affair)…I mean **WELL-ROUNDED WEALTH**, not restricted to just monetary wealth, though they are definitely inter-connected.

You may not yet think it's possible because of your past conditioning, but you CAN have a bursting bank account, a loving family that you spend a lot of time with (if you want to), great friends and a life lived at the stress level of your choosing.

Your life truly is an à la carte menu and the meal's on the house!

(I really don't know what that means, but it sounds profound.)

DOES MONEY EQUAL HAPPINESS?

This is a perfect time to bring up the perennial debate that very few people are actually able to weigh in on from experience.

The answer to the question "Does money equal happiness?" is not as cut and dried as you'd like to hear. Besides you're still going to think that more money WILL make you happier, but here goes:

Money does not equal happiness.

This is a real doozy for most people until they make their first ten million dollars, pinch themselves and then say:

"Huh, nothing feels different. I'm still pissed my dad abandoned us at an early age, I have no sense of who I am now that I sold the company I built investing 80 hours a week of my time in for the past ten years and I still resent my bratty kids because we gave them everything they wanted…and more…and they STILL bark at us like we're servants."

Money does not equal happiness for the simple reason that happiness comes from within and when we peg our own happiness against external benchmarks (like how many dollars we have in the bank or whether our boss pats us on the head and tosses us a treat for a job well done), it is only an *illusion* of happiness because external benchmarks are always moving targets beyond our control.

Happiness, rather, is feeling pride in our work, learning and gaining confidence in our skills and abilities, seeing how we are actually helping others while expecting nothing in return, being lost in the flow of a creative project or making incremental progress toward the goals we care about most.

Happiness has nothing to do with the number of commas in your net worth, but has everything to do with whether you see the abundance in your own life WHEREVER you are and WHEREVER you look and feel genuine gratitude for it.

Right now.

And now.

And now.

What IS true is that money can equal less UNHAPPINESS if by unhappiness you mean stress about how and when the bills are going to be paid and a family's basic needs met month after month and year after year.

But money equaling less UNHAPPINESS is not the same as money equaling HAPPINESS.

I didn't want to believe that money doesn't equal happiness, either, my friend. I STILL occasionally think that I'll be happier when every future financial concern is pulverized by a net worth that I could never spend in this lifetime... forgetting that with financial wealth comes a greater responsibility and a whole new set of concerns.

Think about it for a second. With true financial wealth, suddenly your alma mater is hounding you to fund a building in your name where they can research retinal cancer in frogs, everyone in your family expects you to pay for every dinner out and every vacation together (after the pandemic ends) and ALL your neighbors expect you to donate handsomely to their pet causes...which are often LITERAL pet causes like ending discrimination against purse dogs at the opera.

But the evidence is overwhelming that money does NOT equal happiness from those who have blazed the trail before us.

I can personally attest to a great sense of RELIEF and euphoria when that final student loan payment cleared, but that was an endorphin-fueled rush of a long-term goal being accomplished, not happiness, per se.

Even now when I look at my family's net worth, I feel safety and security, but happiness is not part of the equation – just no stress at the thought of covering a financial emergency.

$$$

Stop what you're doing right now and think, "I have a million dollars in the bank." Or if you want to over-achieve, you little teacher's pet, "I have TEN million dollars in the bank."

Imagine yourself opening a banking app on your phone right now and seeing $1,078,552 just sitting in there. (I gave you a little extra because it's not realistic to see an even $1,000,000. You're welcome.)

How do you feel in this exact moment thinking about that money sitting in there? Do you feel happy…or do you feel relief?

Maybe you would feel happy SPENDING money on yourself or buying gifts for friends and family, but the money itself really just provides a sense of relief, doesn't it? Relief and that feeling of safety and security I keep rambling on about.

When I do this exercise myself, I stop and wait to see what feeling rises within.

For sure there is an adrenaline rush of excitement of "I did it! I knew I could!"

And then, "Suck it, high school bullies!"

(Wow. This just got uncomfortable. Maybe I have a few things from my past to reckon with. But they are probably emotionally miserable if they're still berating others to feel better about themselves so let's just move on.)

But then I wait a few seconds and think, "Okay, but our car still needs to be filled with electricity (c'mon, we live in Los Angeles) and my daughter still needs new clothes because she's growing like a weed and needs to be picked up from school just like every other day. I'm still me, I just now have a little more breathing room to pursue my dreams which are still just as much of a work in progress as I am."

Take as long as you want to daydream about what it would feel like to have a million or ten million buckaroonies to your name. Is it genuine happiness or something else you feel?

$$\$\$\$$$

When you have more money in the bank than you "need," you have to know who you are and what you ultimately want out of life so you can pursue it…or you're going to be just as miserable and unhappy as you were the day before your account ballooned with all that fake money I gave you.

You'd be surprised at how many multimillionaires have found themselves in this same situation – they have more money in the bank than they know what to do with, their lives haven't changed much from before when they DIDN'T have money and they're shocked that they're the same person as the day before. The question that hits them next is, "So NOW what?!?"

In fact, if you talk to millionaires who had always dreamed of hitting the million dollar benchmark, as soon as they reached it, they often felt emotionally let down – many even experienced depression – as the big ticker tape parade welcoming them to the club never happens - they're the same person, just with a fatter net worth.

Todd Tresidder, the man with a helluva first name and the founder of Financial Mentor, often blogs about this very topic. After selling his hedge fund and making enough money to never have to work again, some very interesting things started percolating to the surface for him.

Sure, he took a year off and traveled the world once he became a multi-millionaire, but he soon realized that he no longer had any EXCUSES as to why he was not happy with his life, in whatever area he felt the lack.

He woke up FEELING like the same person he was before the financial windfall, but from that moment forward he didn't have anything or anyone to blame for any unhappiness he felt; as he says, his life had now become self-determined (he could do anything he wanted and create his days however he chose), it was no longer pre-determined (working five or more days of a classic workweek, answering to others, that most everyone can relate to).

With nothing to HAVE to do, he was surprised to find himself 100% responsible for how he felt about his life. And THAT was a major wake-up call for him that we can all learn from...now... before hitting it big.

Of course, once you have more money in the bank than all of your closest friends, good luck getting any sympathy regarding any of life's hardships. We've witnessed this many times behind the backs of people we know who have a net worth in the tens of millions...there is no sympathy from the outside looking in...because people without much money mistakenly assume that MORE money will solve all their problems.

And since they know that more money would make their lives easier (without any proof), they don't want to hear people WITH money bitch about…anything, really.

But you and I know better now, right?

RIGHT?

Remember that what you may create for yourself in financial wealth one day, you will equally lose in sympathy from anyone who has less than you. And them's the breaks.

It's an interesting problem to have and one that is echoed throughout the books and blogs of the newly wealthy.

When we can no longer blame lack of money for our unhappiness, we realize WE must have been at the source of the unhappiness all along!

But you won't believe me that money doesn't equal happiness until you get there so GO FOR IT - chase money and keep telling yourself that once you have *x* million dollars in the bank, then you'll be happy. And when you're still not happy, buy me beers (that plural is not a typo) and we'll chat and figure out where to go from there.

Looking back on my own life, I never felt that my partner and I were going to have any significant money to our names since I carried consumer debt for so long, but now that we will become first-generation millionaires, we can definitely say that we are not any HAPPIER, but we are certainly LESS UNCOMFORTABLE and less stressed in the money department.

As of the tail end of 2021, I have received almost $1.75 million in health care services for the discovery of and treatment for a cancer diagnosis. Multiple myeloma, an incurable blood cancer that lives in the bone marrow – surprise!

Besides making it a real whirlwind of a year, physically and emotionally, one thing that has NOT stressed us out is the financial aspect of it all – we had health insurance in place and have been able to weather the medical bills that continue to roll in with our monthly cash flow.

And the bills keep rolling in – case in point, in mid-December we received a bill from the physician's assistant who delivered the news to me that the MRI turned up "more tumors than the radiologist could count." How much might one pay to hear the worst news of their life? A cool $500 is how much. And due to the incredible (sarcasm) American health care system, that bill showed up exactly 9 months after the date of service – just as we thought we were done with surprises from the Postal Service. Merry Christmas, Todd!

(This story does have a happy-ish ending as that bill had not yet been billed through insurance and it should be covered by the emergency room copay, but HOW MANY

PEOPLE wouldn't think to check on it and would just start paying it?)

The truth is that we were incredibly happy when we had nothing…we learned very early in our relationship that we didn't need to spend money to have fun – just spending time together was what mattered most. Even home-coooked meals were often better than what we'd get at a pricey restaurant.

What money in the bank DOES do is help you sleep at night knowing that the money dam has been tested and that it'll be quite a while before you would ever go thirsty again.

Speaking of The Money Dam, let's take a look at it anew in this little book on wealth.

The Money Dam

I created this years ago and I'm surprised every time I see it at how it helps me to visualize and organize my own thoughts around our finances.

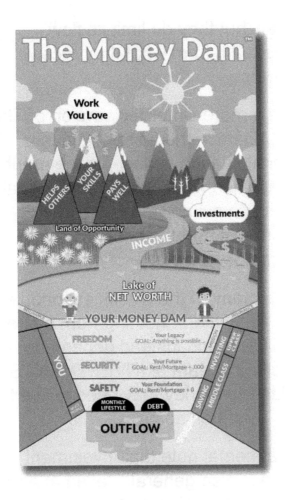

The Money Dam™

Work You Love

HELPS OTHERS   YOUR SKILLS   PAYS WELL

Land of Opportunity

Investments

INCOME

Lake of NET WORTH

YOUR MONEY DAM

FREEDOM   Your Legacy
GOAL: Anything is possible

SECURITY   Your Future
GOAL: Rent/Mortgage + .000

SAFETY   Your Foundation
GOAL: Rent/Mortgage + 0

MONTHLY LIFESTYLE   DEBT

OUTFLOW

Think of the money you have as water behind a dam. Just as dams let water through to generate electricity or to fulfill contracts to provide water downstream, you do this, too, when you pay for anything in your life. The biggest dams don't completely block the flow of water, after all, but they do limit its flow downstream from what they receive upstream.

I used a more simplified version of The Money Dam in the first book in this personal finance series – in the graphic above, when we're talking about wealth, we have to acknowledge the role of investments and their importance in raising a person's lake of net worth.

In fact, many of the wealthiest people make very little or nothing from a stream of INCOME and instead depend on their diversified stream of INVESTMENTS to provide the money they need to live their lives…and then some.

Take a mental note that Investment Income is also generally taxed at a much lower rate than Earned Income from a business or job so it is every reader's goal as they increase their lake of net worth to educate themselves on the intricacies of investment income or to work with professionals who can best advise them on this front.

[This is still a shortened version of The Money Dam. For the free full-color final version and to learn how to use it for your own financial check-in, go to: thinkwealthybook.com]

WOULD YOU RATHER BE RICH OR WEALTHY?

The two words *rich* and *wealthy* are often used somewhat interchangeably, but I want to distinguish one from the other before we move on.

I get it. When others can describe you and your family using either term ('rich' or 'wealthy'), you're not going to care one way or the other, right?

Or as my grandfather would bark out in a loopy diabetic rage, "I don't care what you call me...just don't call me late for dinner!"

Although both *rich* and *wealthy* indicate an abundance of money, there are important distinctions I'd like to make between the two.

Rich is visible. Wealth is discreet.

Someone who is rich may very well show off their *riches* via the clothes they wear, the cars they drive and the home(s) in which they live…whereas the wealthy, who may certainly enjoy all of these things, don't derive their sense of *self* or a sense of satisfaction from the exhibition of these things - they are more modest in outward display.

You can SEE rich people whereas the wealthy aren't big on show.

Wealth does not carry with it the novelty of newfound riches.

If being rich is a statement to some people, being wealthy is an adjective like any other that someone may use to describe a person or family.

Rich is an event. Wealth is a habit.

A rich family is the couple down the street who win the lottery or sell the family business and take home a cool 5 million smackeroos. They won't be wealthy, however, until they turn that 5 million into 10 million because they understand and respect money and make it grow through smart investments to create generational wealth.

It is said that rich people make the news when they get money – wealthy people only make the news when they lose it.

Rich is a number. Wealth is a range.

The rich can more accurately count their money whereas the wealthy have so many assets of ever-changing value that they don't know what their exact net worth is.

I learned this while reading *How To Get Rich* by the late Felix Dennis, a thought-provoking and hilarious tale by one of the world's self-made multimillionaires. He remarked that the truly wealthy can not determine their *own* net worth because of the ever-shifting value of the assets they've parked their money in, not including all the various tax scenarios of cashing out those assets, so they find it quite amusing when the editors of magazines and papers [cough... forbesbloombergwallstreetjournal... cough] peg their net worth with such confidence.

A rich person may be worth 12M, but a wealthy person may be worth anywhere from 200M to 300M on any given day. Heck, Mark Zuckerberg's wealth fluctuated by 3.1B (that's billions) in a single week because so much of his net worth is parked within the somewhat illiquid asset of Facebook company stock. Three billion dollars that was here one day, gone the next!

And then back again. And then gone. And then back again...

That's the reality of so-called paper wealth or when an outsized portion of your portfolio is based in paper assets such as company stock and other market-indexed assets.

As I write this in October of 2021, Jeff Bezos is the richest person in the world with a net worth estimated at $177 billion. Elon Musk is closing in on Jeff with $151 billion and Bernard Arnault rounds out the top three with $150 billion. (Oh, Bernard, how do you even get out of bed in the morning with those kinds of numbers? It's just embarrassing.)

Rich is transient, wealth is enduring.

All of the nouveau millionaire coders and techies in Silicon Valley are rich, but not yet wealthy.

A person or a family who is wealthy implies a sophistication and history with money. The Du Pont family and its heirs are wealthy as is any family that uses their money to set up foundations, erect new buildings on college campuses and fund PBS shows that use the word "verdant" in the intro that sends us all scrambling to our dictionaries.

The wealthy have found the causes they believe in and they are known as major philanthropists within their communities.

The wealthy understand the responsibility to help others that comes with their fortunes whereas the rich may be sitting on a pile of millions like deer in the headlights thinking, "Uhh…I made an app where you flick Cheetos into the bras of sorority girls…I guess I'll take the $10M I made in in-app purchases today to Vegas and…bet it all on red?"

It's a good idea to distinguish the differences between being rich and being wealthy to provide the right context for our conversations together.

Rich and riches denote a certain youth of financial wisdom whereas wealth connotes a longevity or generational quality to it, and an acknowledgment of the responsibility that comes with amassing a sizeable fortune.

The expression of someone being "filthy rich" even highlights the difference I'm trying to make as it makes money feel dirty, greedy and crass, but wealth feels refined, calm and serene…you almost hear classical music playing behind the word "wealth."

In the end, a lot of cash makes you rich, but a lot of money makes you wealthy.

ARE YOU WAITING FOR $UPERMAN?

"C'mon, Todd, why are we even talking about monetary riches or wealth at all? This is the era of social good, being green, leaving the planet a better place for the families we're not creating until our late 30s if at all – 'money' is a dirty word…like 'carbon footprint' or 'vaccination.' And don't even get me started on the global pandemic that has devastated millions of households around the globe!"

Yes! But money is important, and always will be, and always has been, because it is as life-sustaining as water is for your body. But I hear you. I feel you. (Heck, I'm the one who just wrote that!)

If we never take charge and manage our money so that it provides a level of safety and security for us and for our family, we will always be dependent on handouts from others (bosses, our credit cards/banks, friends, the government) to get by.

There was an eye-opening documentary about the American educational system in 2010 called *Waiting for "Superman"* that followed several children as they attempted to make it into their local charter school, their best chance at pulling themselves and their families out of poverty through a good education. It is a very compelling film.

It was titled *Waiting for "Superman"* based on one of the educators in the film recounting how frightened he was to learn as a kid that Superman was a fictional character (spoiler alert) who was NOT coming to save him and his family after all. The realization that it was up to him to be the change he wanted to see in the world was a sobering and defining moment in his life.

With Social Security now acting as the major source of income for most of the elderly in this country, we ALL need to wake up to the fact that there is no financial Superman (or $uperman) coming to save US, either.

$uperman does not exist. He is not going to fly in to fully fund your Roth IRA for the next five years nor will he pop out of a local phone booth (a what?) to rescue you from any reverse compounding interest you're paying to a credit card company.

The sooner we get this into our heads and understand what that means, the sooner we can take action to make sure we, too, are not dependent on the federal government to pay our basic bills in our latter years.

Re-TIRED-ment

What went "wrong?" Why are so many people dependent on Social Security well into their golden years?

Two answers:

1) We're living longer than we ever have.

If you retire at 65, there's a good chance you'll live for another 30 years. 30 years!

Yet you were only in the workforce for 45 years (if you work from ages 20 to 65) so in those 45 years of generating an income you needed to be saving and investing enough to live during the final 30 years when you're not producing an income – basically every year and a half of employment needs to fund an entire year of life post-retirement!

2) The traditional financial blueprint for a happy retirement has changed.

A successful retirement used to consist of a three-pronged financial approach: a company pension, personal savings and Social Security. With pensions having mainly gone the way of the dodo bird, that three-legged stool is now a two-legged stool: savings and Social Security, yet 62% of us don't even have $1,000 in savings so most people are sitting on a one-legged stool!

Have you ever sat on a one-legged stool? It's called a pole and it hurts when shoved up your caboose.

In essence, the first leg, **pensions**, became too expensive for corporations to maintain while continuing to show ever-increasing profits for their shareholders so Congress came up with the company 401(k) "defined-contribution plan" in 1978 – that pushed the responsibility of the primary leg of retirement income onto the shoulders of the employee – YOU!

Thanks, Congress!

That 401(k) your company offers *is* your pension – but now you're in charge of funding it and nurturing it up through retirement.

Even the "safe" pensions that still exist today are routinely gutted and raided when the corporations, cities and institutions that fund them realize they have big bills due today and so they grab from tomorrow's dollars which were already promised to someone else.

For the second leg of retirement planning, **personal savings**, wages have not increased over the past few decades beyond keeping pace with inflation or the general rise in the cost of living. With no real gain in middle-class wages for 30 years (which is a crime in itself) there is no extra income to set aside for a healthy savings account.

What about the third leg of the stool – **Social Security**?

Not surprisingly, nowadays Social Security is the major source of income for most of the elderly in this country, a burden for which it was never intended.

We hear all the time about the impending demise of Social Security and that it may not make it to the day when our children are retiring, but it seems unrealistic that it will simply run out of money one day. Steps will *probably* be taken to keep it solvent for the long haul once it becomes a crisis that can no longer be ignored by our elected officials – but, for the sake of this discussion, let's assume that Social

Security WILL be there as a sturdy-ish stool leg.

Any way you slice it, the onus of retirement has been transferred from the corporation into the money-uneducated hands of the employee/consumer...YOU. And ME.

The bold truth everyone is facing now is that we are completely in charge of our own financial future. And...

No one is going to fly in and save you financially.

There is no $uperman.

And there never will be. Even if you inherited a majestic sum of money or came into a sizeable windfall, it's still up to you to manage it and make it last through your remaining trips around the sun.

This is not meant to scare you – you make all the choices in your life the same as everyone else.

It's just a reality check so you understand that you have plenty of options beyond the shaky Social Security check from the U.S. government. Which isn't a very sizeable monthly check, anyway.

Revisiting the fact that the United States is the wealthiest nation in the history of the world, doesn't it sound totally *ridonks* that the majority of the elderly depend on THEIR GOVERNMENT to keep them financially afloat (and even then just barely!) through the last years of their lives?

I'm not okay with that for me and my family. I will not be an elderly child waiting for my allowance each month from my overly-bureaucratic, bipolar (Democrat/Republican) and…let's call a fig a fig and a trough a trough…total creeper of a dude Uncle Sam.

Regardless of what the future of Social Security looks like, in my own family we are fully planning to save and invest enough to create strong cash flow from our assets to keep us spending and enjoying our lives all the way to our dirt naps.

What surprised us…and may surprise you, too…is that it only took us about 2 years of aggressive funding to build up our retirement reserves due to the power of compounding interest and the time we have left until we need to tap those funds. That is true for everyone – the sooner you start investing, the less you need to set aside!

Since there is no one coming to save us with a big bucket of money, that gives us a few options:

A) We can learn to like the taste of cat food for our stay at the state-run Crusty Roach Motel and Convalescent Home.

B) We can marry someone super-rich in a community property state and kick and scream against signing a pre-nup.

C) We can dive head-first into the super simple Wealth Equation that every wealthy person knows by heart to create the financial safety and security we crave.

I hope you'll agree that C is the obvious solution here.

The great news it that it doesn't matter how old you are as it's NEVER too late to turn things around.

N.E.V.E.R

The Wealth Equation doesn't require a long time horizon or a lot of money, it only requires a strong desire to turn things around.

THE ONLY WEALTH EQUATION YOU EVER NEED TO LEARN

Hear ye. Hear ye.

There will only ever be ONE AND ONLY ONE financial formula you need to know to become as wealthy as your heart desires. And it is so fundamental that even our distant cavemen forefathers figured it out.

Heck, even other species understand this universal law – it's why squirrels store nuts for the winter, dogs bury bones and on and on and on.

The next time you look at your credit card statement and shake your head because you can barely make the minimum payment, call Rover over for some solid financial advice.

No wealthy person in the world has EVER become wealthy without this magical formula:

EARN > SPEND

Earn more than you spend. That's all you need. I even made the SPEND side a little smaller to drive it home graphically.

There it is, folks!

You may know this more commonly as SPEND < EARN (spend less than you earn). It's the same equation, but we're talking about the <u>creation</u> <u>of</u> <u>wealth</u> and you can always EARN more because money is abundant, but there does come a point where you can't spend any less, so I flip-flopped the equation for emphasis on the EARNING side.

Notice the wealth equation is not EARN = SPEND which is living paycheck to paycheck or EARN < SPEND which is why many people are up to their eyeballs in debt.

No, my friend, there are only two sides to the equation to work with.

Now let's all say it with different emphasis each time.

So. That. We. All. GET. It.

EARN more than you spend.

Earn MORE than you spend.

Earn more than you SPEND.

Integrate this into your daily DNA and money will start rising up in your bank accounts like water behind your own Money Dam. You will never go broke if you follow this equation.

Which is why I say:

Earn more than you spend – dam it!

It's the most powerful equation that exists for creating the safety, security and freedom that a rising net worth can provide to you and your family.

Even in retirement you need to earn more than you spend because you don't know how long you'll live and this wealth-building equation will help keep you feeling safe and secure even as you transition back into diapers. (Ever the financial poet laureate am I.)

Our Only Financial Job in Life

A reminder to us all that we really only have one financial job in our lifetime and that is to pay our bills every MONTH until game over.

That's it!

As I've said before…

Financially-speaking, our only job is to pay our monthly bills.

I don't care how many millions of dollars you may have in the bank one day, you will always have MONTHLY bills to pay and if you always have MORE coming in than is GOING OUT each month, you will always feel safe.

We have the Ancient Egyptians to thank for this monthly bill-paying cycle because they decided to measure time by tracking the sun across the sky instead of the moon. Which is win-win for you and me because on a moon-based lunar calendar we'd have an EXTRA month of bills every 2 to 3 years – nooooooo thank you!

But that's it. Our only real financial job is to ensure our monthly cash flow for life – if we want to feel wealthy, all we have to do is simply bring in more than we spend each month and invest the rest.

See how easy life is?!?

THE HOW OF MODERN WEALTH

Now that we know the only wealth equation you ever need to learn (which is no big surprise to anyone who's managed their money on their own, but still it had to be said in a simplified form), how do we achieve wealth in our own lives? That's what we're REALLY talking about, isn't it?

Let's first take a look at how the accumulation of wealth has changed over the years.

In the great American heyday, with the arrival of the Industrial Age and the westward expansion across North America, there was endless opportunity to provide products and services that a growing superpower needed. Many of the men (you guessed it, across the board they were all straight, white men...to the best of our knowledge) who made fortunes for themselves and their families still sound familiar to modern ears in the institutions and buildings that their wealth has left behind.

Ever been to New York City and taken in a concert at Carnegie Hall? Or toured the campus of Carnegie Mellon University in Pittsburgh? Did you know that J. D. Rockefeller helped to found (and fund) the University of Chicago along with The Rockefeller University, also in NYC? Of course, Vanderbilt University should ring a bell, too.

All the captains of industry from America's Gilded Age like DuPont (gunpowder, textiles), Rockefeller (oil), Vanderbilt (steamships, railroads), Ford (automobiles), Carnegie (steel) and Mellon (coal, aluminum) sat at the top of the industrial and manufacturing food chain – they owned the businesses that the growing American empire (and rest of the world) relied upon.

There were also incredibly wealthy financiers and investors like J. P. Morgan whose legacy remains with us today in the form of JPMorgan Chase & Co. (a.k.a. Chase bank).

Of course, this is the cream of the crop whose fortunes rivaled today's billionaires when you account for inflation. But back in the day they were just millionaires. (Just.)

Fun fact: The world's first billionaire was actually John D. Rockefeller who earned the "big B" title in 1916 primarily through his ownership stake in Standard Oil. Since then there has been no turning back the financial pissing contest and the public's fascination with the ever-lengthening list of billionaires.

Another fun fact: America's first self-made female millionaire was Madam C.J. Walker (born Sarah Breedlove), a Black woman and entrepreneur who revolutionized the black hair-care industry – her assets were valued at over one million dollars at the time of her death in

1919. Her products are still available today at Sephora!

Third fun fact (and then I'll leave you alone): The first self-made female billionaire was Marth Stewart who achieved that title in 2000 after taking her company, Martha Stewart Living Omnimedia, public a year earlier in 1999.

A Million vs. a Billion

It's so easy to mistake the proximity of a million dollars to a billion dollars. They even sound like close cousins! But someone who has a net worth of one MILLION dollars is leagues apart from someone who has a net worth of one BILLION dollars in terms of underlying financial assets.

We know this conceptually – a billion is a thousand millions, of course – but the numbers are so large and foreign to most people when they look at their Mint or Personal Capital account...or ATM balance if that's where they keep the majority of their net worth…the numbers are so alien to us that "million" and "billion" start to sound the same.

A post went viral on Twitter a few years back when @Paul_Franz tweeted that "people don't have a strong intuitive sense of how much bigger 1 billion is than 1 million. 1 million seconds is about 11 days. 1 billion seconds is about 31.5 years."

Whoa. That's a big difference.

Stated another way, if you spent $1 every second a millionaire will run out of money in about 11 days, but if you spent $1 every second a billionaire will run out of money in about 31.5 years.

There is a WHOPPING difference between 11 days and 31 years!

A billion dollars feels almost obscene in this context.

I drove my daughter to school yesterday and I passed by a small local church pulling together what looked a dozen crates of donated food for distribution. This feels like two different planets I'm talking about, basic food distribution versus this current talk of millionaires and billionaires. That being said, who knows if a local, wealthy-ish benefactor didn't make a sizeable donation to that church to keep it operational and able to support its local community.

So let the record show that a net worth of a **billion** dollars is wildly more abundant (and some might say excessive) than a net worth of a **million** dollars.

Millionaires vs. Billionaires in the US

For the sake of simplicity, I'm going to keep the stats to the US population because it's the country with the most of each.

Although these numbers are always shifting:

Billionaires: There are about 614 billionaires in the US.

Millionaires: There are over 20 million millionaires in the US.

Those numbers alone show us how much "easier" it is to achieve a net worth of over one million dollars in assets in a person or family's lifetime than it is to join the billionaire's club.

The fact of the matter is that you can SAVE your way to a million dollars of net worth within one lifetime. Yes, it would take a high-paying job and a frugal lifestyle once you factor in the cost of being taxed on earned income, but it's possible.

What's easier, and how most Americans achieve millionaire status, is through a combination of saving (the lowest tier of The Money Dam which we do to feel Safe) and investing (the middle tier of The Money Dam which we do to feel Secure).

Most Americans sock away money into tax-advantaged retirement accounts so their money can grow at an average (and I do mean average given the wild fluctuations in the financial markets over the years) annual rate of return of 8%. They also own real estate assets: a home and possibly a secondary investment property that historically will appreciate over time. Their track to a net worth of more than a million dollars is pretty pedestrian and typically low-risk.

They look like you and me because they ARE you and me.

Anyone who has reached a net worth of a billion dollars, however, has done so almost exclusively through owning so-called paper assets in the form of securities. Elon Musk, Jeff Bezos, Mark Zuckerberg and Bill Gates are synonymous with the companies they created. Their wealth and net worth are intimately tied to the stock they own in the corporations they currently run or once ran.

Billionaire investors also created their wealth through holding securities: Warren Buffett, Carl Icahn, Ray Dalio, George Soros, John Paulson. Mark Cuban first became a billionaire with the sale of Broadcast.com but has since multiplied his net worth via his investments in other businesses.

You can also become a billionaire through owning real estate, but there are far fewer real estate investors in the B Club and they did it primarily by developing commercial, as opposed to residential, real estate. Their names don't show up in the media as often, but perhaps you've heard of Sam Zell, Stephen Ross or Donald Bren. Los Angelenos have all pretty much heard of billionaire Rick Caruso since many of us have shopped or dined at one of his outdoor shopping centers: The Grove or The Americana.

I'm stating the obvious, but there is simply no way to save your way into the billionaire's club – you must own assets that have almost no ceiling, or cap, to their potential growth.

Unless you have the luxury of time ahead of you and an unstoppable work ethic (or an already-wealthy parent in your family tree who you BETTER be nice to), there are probably few, if any, future billionaires reading this book – they're already out there experimenting and testing their ideas in the marketplace.

The rest of you will just have to be happy living as multi-millionaires.

But prove me wrong – go make a billion dollars and then give back to the world to leave it a better place than you found it. We dare you!

What is Wealth in 2021?

Financial services company Charles Schwab released their 2021 Modern Wealth Survey after polling 1,000 people to see what they "think about saving, spending, investing and wealth" and their results are quite interesting.

What's interesting is how ACHIEVABLE many of these numbers are with even a low-risk investment strategy. Here's what they found…

In terms of Average Net Worth:

To be considered **wealthy,** respondents felt $1.9M was sufficient (DOWN from $2.6M in 2020).

For **financial happiness,** respondents felt $1.1M was enough (DOWN from $1.75M in 2020).

To be **financially comfortable,** respondents felt $624K filled the bill (DOWN from $934K in 2020).

Differentiating between financial happiness and financial comfortability feels a bit nebulous, but what surprised me, overall, is how LOW these numbers are. Maybe my living in Los Angeles for several decades has skewed my perception of what it means to "have money," but most people I know wouldn't consider themselves wealthy with a net worth of two million dollars.

What do YOU think? Are these numbers in line with your thinking or do you have higher financial aspirations?

THE ONE THING YOU HAVE IN COMMON WITH ALL WEALTHY PEOPLE

Buckle up…here's the one thing that YOU have in common with all rich and wealthy people.

Are you ready for this amazing nugget of truthosity? I've studied this for decades – invested a lot of my time into this!

What the wealthy all have in common is…

Nothing.

Oh wait, let me double-check my facts.

I see, I was wrong, yes, what the wealthy actually all have in common is...

Absolutely nothing.

(Pregnant pause to let that sink in...and then the baby is born.)

How liberating to learn that the wealthy don't have anything in common, right?

Personally, I thought I had to have a brilliant mind to be wealthy.

You don't need to be a genius to be wealthy.

I thought wealthy people gathered together at their secret hideaway mountain lairs and pulled up a picture of me on some high-tech, spendy hologram device, studied my profile and then all shook their heads in unison while mumbling to one another, "That poor soul. If only he were a *little* bit smarter...if he just read one more book...if he'd just

finished all the articles on the internet…
then he could play in all of our amazing
reindeer games. But alas, the Fates have
cursed him with too few noggin neurons."

Then they would all break into laughter.

I got great grades in school and generally
feel smarter than the average bear (don't
we all…thereby leaving no average bear
left…just all of us thinking we're smarter
than everyone else?), but I have never
considered myself to be too much of a
brainiac.

Which is good news for me – and us!

The rich and wealthy are not any smarter
than you.

In fact, in the Forbes 400 of the richest
Americans, only 21 out of 400 completed
an academic Ph.D. That is, just 5.25%, of
the richest Americans have a Ph.D.

Those are terrible odds if you're hoping
those three letters and two periods at the
end of your name will make you wealthy.

There are other reasons why higher academic degrees are not prevalent among the financially prosperous, one of them being that masters and doctorate degrees have only risen to higher prominence in the past couple of decades, long after many of the billionaires on the list had already begun their financial journeys.

This was always my biggest mistake, though - I assumed everyone who is super-rich is brilliant beyond compare and that if I just had more formal education or read more books and magazines, I could get my brain ready for the day when it would crank out amazing money-making ideas.

What IS true is that the wealthy are often experts within their niches of specialization. It doesn't mean that they are generally brilliant Jeopardy!-winning individuals, but that they probably know their field of business forward and backward. And forward again.

I had always been told to go to school, get good grades and then get a good job.

Obviously, the more education I crammed into my cranium, the higher my net worth, right?

You don't even need a formal education to be wealthy.

Out of those same top 400 wealthiest Americans, 63 of them, or 16%, have no college degree. 9% of them dropped out of college and the other 7% finished high school but never attended college.

So you don't *technically* need a formal education to be wealthy, although you certainly seem to increase your odds if you do have one as 40% of the richest Americans *did* finish college and another 40% finished grad school, some of them earning multiple degrees.

Don't let this fact dissuade you from getting a degree as higher education has played a role in the vast majority of the country's wealthiest families, but also don't let it discourage you if college doesn't appeal to you and your parents are on board with you rolling the secondary education dice.

Speaking of rolling the dice...

You don't need to be lucky to be wealthy.

We'll take all of the luck we can get our hands on, but most of the wealthy agree that people create their own luck by always being on the lookout for opportunities, taking calculated risks and trusting that they can always deliver value for others.

It's true that some wealthy individuals consider themselves positively drenched in the saliva of Lady Luck (financial poet laureate in the house)...but let's not use feeling like a lucky or unlucky person as an excuse for not even trying.

Go MAKE your luck, my friend.

You don't need to be a greedy, Type A personality to be wealthy.

This is an idea that has been created and supported by so many representations in pop culture and in the media – the mega corporation headed by the evil Mr. Burns, Gordon Gekko in *Wall Street*, the greedy old Mr. Scrooge of Christmas lore, Logan Roy of *Succession* fame – the concept that only greedy, bossy people who will step on whomever they can to get ahead is ubiquitous.

Every good story is rooted in conflict and to create conflict you have to have both a clear protagonist and antagonist. In this paradigm, you can see how easy it is to take potshots at those in power, at those with more relative wealth than the protagonist. The wealthy and powerful seem untouchable because they've achieved what so many others have only dreamed of.

Don't believe it for a second.

Of course, some of the richest and wealthiest people in the world are greedy and some of them are larger-than-life... egomaniacs....because why? What have we learned?

Money just makes you more of who you already are.

Because money is 100% neutral.

There are just as many generous, introverted wealthy individuals and families out there so don't let this one hold you back - it's an excuse like any other.

Confession

I have a confession.

I lied earlier when I said the wealthy don't have anything in common. (And here you were just beginning to trust me – suckas!)

The wealthy do have one thing in common.

It's just not the traditional things that we think about.

The wealthy all believe that they are WORTHY of wealth.

The wealthy all believe they deserve to be wealthy.

I don't mean they feel they deserve it without working for it, but the wealthy all know they are worthy and capable of the *responsibility* of handling whatever amount of money they collect behind their money dams. In that sense, they know they deserve to be wealthy.

The truly wealthy are good stewards of money. They accept the responsibility and don't take it lightly.

This is the single greatest differentiator between the haves and the have-nots. Most people would say, just like my mom, "What would I even DO with a million dollars? I don't NEED that much."

They're confusing wealth with materialism and think they are being asked to SPEND the million dollars.

They don't yet understand that:

Money is just a tool that provides safety, security and freedom for

yourself and others.

For the wealthy, when an opportunity comes along and says, "Hi Mr. and Mrs. Wealthy Persons, for x amount of time and/or $ of investment, I may have millions to give away down the line, now who would like to hear more about it?"

The rich and the wealthy all raise their hands.

These are the same opportunities not even seen by others, not necessarily because they didn't have the same access to them, but because of how they *think* – opportunities are routinely missed by people who are stuck in their heads, subconsciously, about how much they are or are not worth.

The wealthy say, "Yes, please! And if there's any overflow of opportunity (and money) that needs a safe and respectable home, I'll take that, too – dam it!"

So how did the rich and wealthy get to the point that they feel they deserve to be there?

Fundamentally, they all THINK similarly about money, perhaps differently from the way you do now. But that's all – they THINK differently and then act on it!

And when you learn to think the same way, you will be on the road to your own definition of wealth.

It all starts with your mindset which is zipping around up in that beautiful melon attic called your brain.

SUMMARY

Part of helping you to choose the way you view the world is understanding these key concepts covered in this book:

- Wealth is abundance in whatever form it takes – financially-speaking, there is no shortage of money in the world or value being provided to earn that money.

- Wealth and materialism are two completely separate things. Having more money and spending more money do not go hand-in-hand.

- Money does not equal happiness but it can equal less stress…or less unhappiness.

- Being rich and being wealthy are two different animals. Riches imply new money while wealth implies sound money habits and sincere philanthropy across the generations.

- There is no financial $uperman who is going to figure out your finances for you until game over. We are all responsible for building our money dams as high as we can and it is never too late to get started.

- There is, and only ever will be, one Wealth Equation which is Earn > spend. If you simply earn more than you spend every month for the rest of your life, you will always be wealthy because you will never run out of financial resources.

- You build your mental money dam as high as you can by always Earning more than you Spend (E > s) and understanding that money flows to value. Money doesn't discriminate on who has it or who gets it. Earn more than you spend, dam it!

- The only thing all wealthy people have in common is that they know they are worthy of, or deserve, financial wealth and that they will take good care of it. They are not smarter, more educated, luckier or greedier than anyone else – they simply view money as an asset, not as income, that can grow into more money over time.

CPSIA information can be obtained
at www.ICGtesting.com
Printed in the USA
LVHW050341210423
744868LV00002B/124